Let′s Learn Basic Programming in

Enjoyable Way

Chinthaka Premachandra Ph.D

Let's Learn Basic

Programming in Enjoyable Way

(English Edition)

Chinthaka Premachandra Ph.D

Content

Introduction

Many students have limited skills in using programming languages and writing programs. However, as with any new skill, you will improve gradually if you practice constantly. This also applies to programming. As with other subjects, if you do not desist and start learning from the simple basics, you will be able to turn programming into one of your best subjects.

The basics of all programming languages are, to a certain extent, similar, and if you learn one language properly, you can easily learn other languages. This guide explains the basics of programming based on Decimal BASIC, which can be used by anyone at no cost. Moreover, because this guide analyzes Decimal BASIC in a manner that is easy to understand based on appropriate examples, it will facilitate learning for beginners.

This publication is intended for any programming language novice, but is aimed in particular at first and second year university students, and middle and high school students.

About the author

Name

Chinthaka Premachandra (Ph.D)

Affiliation

Department of Electrical Engineering

Faculty of Engineering Division I

Tokyo University of Science, Tokyo, Japan

1. Installing & uninstalling Decimal BASIC

1.1 Installing

Decimal BASIC can be used in different environments, including Windows, Mac, and Linux. This guide explains installation and programming in Windows 7 and Windows 8. Decimal BASIC can be installed in earlier versions than the Windows 8 version following similar procedures. If an old version of Decimal BASIC is already installed, uninstall it and then install the new version. Uninstalling is explained in Section 1.2.

The most recent version of the Decimal BASIC software can be downloaded from the Internet. Using Google, search for "Decimal BASIC install" to quickly find a site from which to download the program. A site currently used often is listed in the References section under [1].

Right-click the downloaded file, and in the window that appears, click "Next (N)".

Click "Next (N)" in the window that appears next.

Enter your user information in the window that appears, and click "Next (N)". You can also proceed without entering any information.

In the next window, you can set an installation destination. If the destination that appears automatically in the window is fine, click "Next (N)".

To install the software in a different location, click "Change (C)", and set a different destination. When you are done, click "Next (N)" .

In the next window, you may select the top or the middle option. If you select the top option, a shortcut is created on the desktop, as indicated in the window. Click "Next (N)" to proceed to the next window, and then click "Install (I)" to install the program. Click "Finish (F)" in the last window to complete the installation.

1.2 Uninstalling

To uninstall, from the Start screen, select Control Panel → Uninstall a program → Decimal BASIC, and then click "Uninstall" .

To install a new version of Decimal BASIC, we highly recommend uninstalling first an already installed older version, and then installing the newer version.

2. Explaining the programming window

Your installed BASIC program is listed in the program list from the Windows Start window, but it is easier to place a shortcut in the desktop.

When you click "BASIC", the programming window shown in Fig. 2.1 appears.

Fig. 2.1 Programming window

As shown in Fig. 2.1, this window has various menus, including File, Edit, and Run, and each of these has a number of functions. This section explains the functions that are often required.

18

2.1 File functions

Fig. 2.2 File functions

As seen in Fig. 2.2, when you click "File", a list of functions appears. These functions include ones that are similar to those in commonly used software, such as Word.

When you click "New", you can open a new program. The window that appears is the same as the window that appears when you run BASIC. When creating a program, close that window, and use this method to open a new program.

Use "Open" to load a program already saved. To load a program, click "Open", select the destination of the program you want to load, and then select the program's source file.

"Close" terminates the program you are currently creating, and is used when you want to stop working on it. On such occasions, you must close the program after saving it. Saving is explained in the next section. By using "Close", you can discontinue working without the programming window disappearing.

Use "Save" to save a program under the name its original name. Use "Save as" to save a program under a new name. If you have opened a new program, you can save it using "Save as". Then, you either select or create a destination, and specify a filename for the new program.

Use "Print" to print the program you are creating. Clicking "Print" displays the window shown in Fig. 2.3. You can set the printer by clicking "Printer setting", and then set the print font by clicking "Font".

Use "Exit BASIC" to terminate your work. To keep the current program, you must save it before exiting.

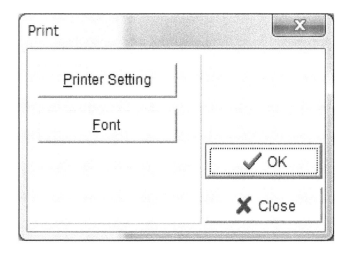

Fig. 2.3 Print window

Fig. 2.4 Tool bar explanation

The functions described above are also included in the tool bar. The buttons circled by the dotted line in Fig. 2.4 are, from left to right, "New", "Open", "Save", and "Print", and you can operate them simply by clicking them.

2.2 Edit functions

Fig. 2.5 shows the Edit functions. Because almost all functions are similar to common software, for instance, Word, individuals familiar with such software can easily use these Edit functions.

Use "Cut" to cut all or part of a program you are creating. Select the portion you want to cut, and then click "Cut". As in Word, select by placing the cursor at the start of the string you want to select, click the left mouse button, and while holding the left mouse button, move the mouse.

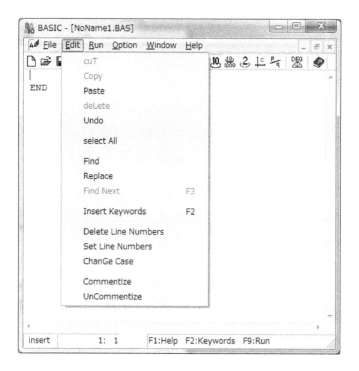

Fig. 2.5 Edit functions

Use "Copy" to copy all or part of a program you are creating. In this case, select the portion you want to copy and click "Copy".

Use "Paste" to paste a string you have either cut or copied. Simply place your mouse cursor on the location you want to paste the string, and click "Paste". As will be explained later, you can also cut or copy strings created in Notepad or Word, and paste them in the programming window.

Use "Delete" when you want to delete strings, etc. in the window. Simply select the string you want to delete and click "Delete".

Use "Undo" to return the status of the programming window to the status of the previous step.

The Edit functions described above are also included in the tool bar. The buttons circled by the dotted line in Fig. 2.6 are, from left to right, "Cut", "Copy", "Paste", and "Undo", and you can operate them simply by clicking them. You can also select the operations described above by right-clicking the mouse.

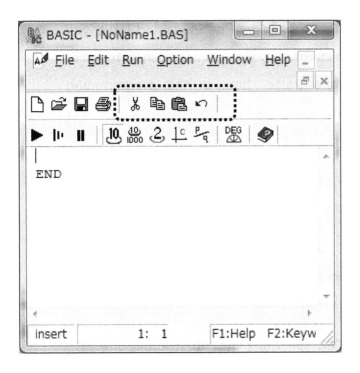

Fig. 2.6 Tool bar explanation

By using the "Search" function, you can search for words or characters in a program. The search function is particularly helpful when creating long programs. Clicking "Search" displays the Search window shown in Fig. 2.7.

Enter the word or string you want to search, and click "Find" on the top right corner, to start the search. If the search term exists multiple times in the program, click this button successively.

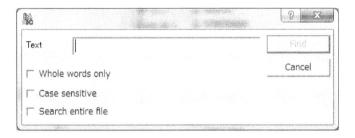

Fig. 2.7 Search window

Use "Replace" to replace one word in your program with another. Clicking "Replace" displays the Replace window shown in Fig. 2.8. Enter the word to be replaced in "Text", and enter the replacement word in "Replace". If replacing all simultaneously, click "Replace

All". If replacing individually, click "Replace" successively.

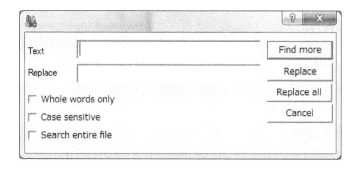

Fig. 2.8 Replace window

By clicking "Add Line Numbers", you can add line numbers. Clicking this displays the window shown in Fig. 2.9. Enter the desired initial and increment, and then click "OK" to attach numbers to each line in the program.

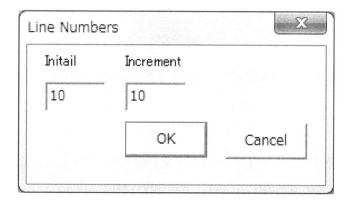

Fig. 2.9 Line number settings screen

Programs work well without line numbers. However, given that adding line numbers to long programs facilitates their analysis, we recommended adding line numbers when writing long programs. To facilitate analysis, line numbers have been added to all the programs in this guide.

Use "Change case" to change font to uppercase or lowercase. Clicking "Change case" displays the window shown in Fig. 2.10, where you can change the font of function names and keywords to uppercase or lowercase. For general use, the settings shown in Fig. 2.10 are fine, but you might want to change such settings to a more convenient form. To make a change, select the desired option in the window and click "OK".

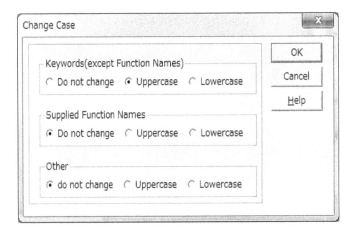

Fig. 2.10 Case settings window

2.3 Run functions

Figure 2.11 shows the Run functions. These include "Run", "Step", and "Break".

"Run" is a function to run the program you have created. When you click "Run", the program is executed.

Use "Step" to run the program step-by-step.

Use "Break" to stop the program before the program finishes execution. "Run", "Step", and "Break" are explained in detail in Example 3.2 in the next chapter. The same operations are possible using the buttons. Try to find the appropriate bottoms for 'Run' and 'Step'.

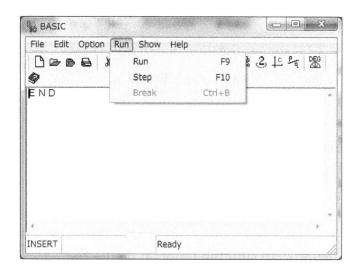

Fig. 2.11 Run functions

2.4 Option functions

As shown in Fig. 2.12, clicking "Option" displays the Option functions.

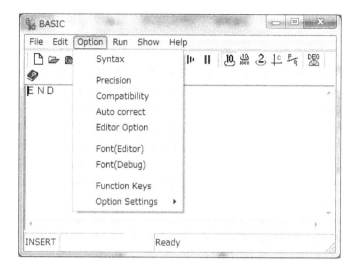

Fig. 2.12 Option functions

"Syntax" is a function to select programming language syntax. Clicking "Syntax" ' displays the Syntax window shown in Fig. 2.13. Using the "Standard" usually causes no problems, but if you run a program written in Microsoft BASIC, you must select Microsoft BASIC Compatible. In such a case, select this option and click "OK".

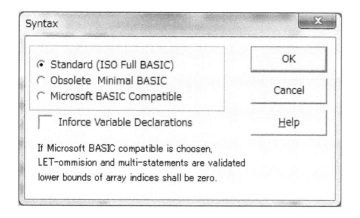

Fig. 2.13 Syntax window

"Numerals" (not available in Fig. 2.12, however some versions includes this function) is a function to set numeral precision. Clicking "Numerals" displays the window shown in Fig. 2.14. If "Decimal 15 digits" is selected, a program calculation results appear with 15 decimal digits. You can change this by selecting your preferred option and clicking "OK" . For general use, the "Decimal 15 digits" setting is fine. Because this function is included in the tool bar, it is easy to use.

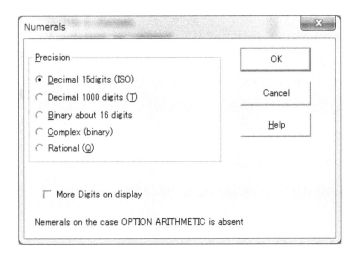

Fig. 2.14 Numeral precision window

Because "Compatibility", and "Auto correct", under Option are not required when writing a program, an explanation for these is not included in this guide. Basically, the settings for these options are fine as they are.

Use "Font (Editor)" to change the font displayed onscreen when writing a program. This changes when the program is run.

"Function Keys" can be used to register the words used more frequently when writing a program, such as PRINT. Clicking "Function Keys" displays the window shown in Fig. 2.15. Set your desired words by entering them and clicking "OK" . When you hold the specified Function key and the Shift key in the programming window, the word appears automatically. This is a handy function to write often-used words.

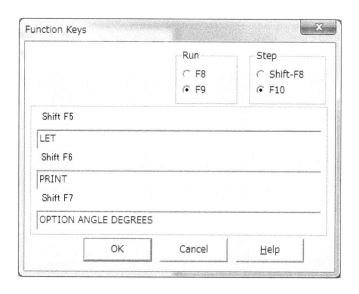

Fig . 2.15 Function Keys setting window

2.5 Show functions

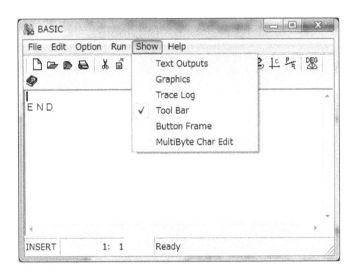

Fig. 2.16 Show functions

The first five "Show" functions displayed in Fig. 2.16 are output windows when running a program. You can ignore these.

If "Tool bar" is selected, the tool bar is displayed. Deselecting it removes the tool bar from your screen. The tool bar is convenient for operations such as running a program, so leave it selected.

When "Button Frame" is selected, the tool bar Button Frame appears neatly displayed.

Use "Tile" and "Cascade" to remove the text input window from the overall screen.

If you use the functions described above when writing programs, you should soon become familiar with them. In the next chapter, we build an actual program. We aim to start simple and gradually boost your level, even if you are not skilled at programming. Starting simple means it will be fun!

3. Formulas, variables, INPUT, PRINT

3.1 Numerical expressions

* Addition, subtraction, multiplication, and division are expressed, respectively, as +, -, *, and /.

* 2^3 is expressed as 2^3.

By entering the calculation you want to perform in PRINT, general calculations can be performed. Simply stated, entering calculations works similarly to a calculator. Try to run the program Example 3.1.

Example 3.1

```
10 PRINT 6+3*4^2

20 PRINT 7/4*5
```

```
30 PRINT 2^4

40 PRINT 1/3

50 END
```

The program input is shown in Fig. 3.1, and Fig. 3.2 shows the results, which are shown with a maximum of 15 digits. To change the number of digits, click Option → Numerals to increase the number of digits. Setting the number of digits is also explained in Chapter 7.

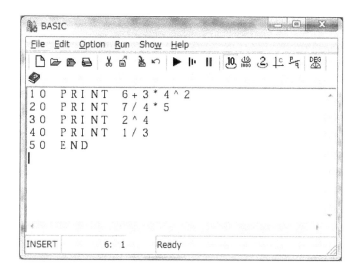

Fig. 3.1 Created program

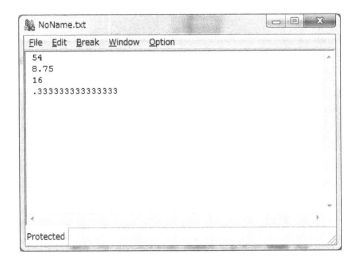

Fig. 3.2 Execution results

* **Brackets (parentheses): complex calculations are no problem if you put brackets in the appropriate places. Example 3.2 shows a calculation with brackets.**

Example 3.2

```
PRINT ((1+3)*4)^2
PRINT 3*(-5)
END
```

Problem 3.1

Try to calculate the following:

(1) $(7.5 \times 50) \div 40$ (2) $250 \div 3 \times (9 - 2)$

Run Example 3.2 using the "Step" function. Figs. 3.3, 3.4, and 3.5 show the screens for running the steps. An explanation of Fig. 3.3 is as follows.

To run a program step-by-step, select "Step" and click "OK" to continue. The bottom three buttons also allows you to use operations such as Undo. To stop the program, either select "Cancel" and click "OK", or click "Abort". You can do the same by simply pressing Esc on your keyboard.

By clicking "Break Points", you can set break points in a program. All programming languages have this type of function, and making good use

of it helps to find bugs easily when programming.
Figs. 3.4 and 3.5 show the execution results to
the current step and the program content,
respectively.

Fig. 3.3 Stepped execution window 1

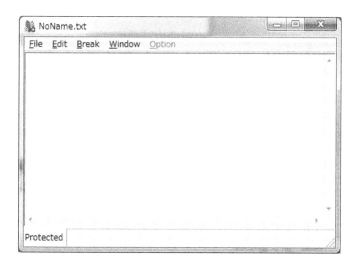

Fig. 3.4 Stepped execution window 2

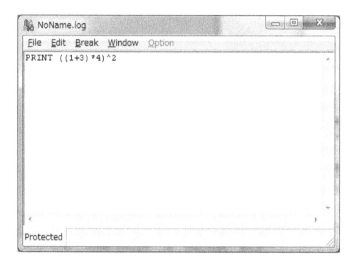

Fig. 3.5 Stepped execution window 3

If you build a program by testing the operations described above, you should soon get familiar with such operations.

3.2 Variables

* When computers "handle" numerals, these are stored in Variables, which are used under names such as A, B, or C. Naturally, variables with multiple characters, such as ABC or CDF, can be used as well.

* Both uppercase and lowercase fonts can be used. Depending on the programming language, uppercase variables can be handled differently from lowercase variables.

* If a variable is substituted with a new numeral mid-program, the numeral maintained to that point disappears and cannot be referred to any longer.

Example 3.3

```
10 LET X=10

20 PRINT 2*X^2+3*X+4

30 LET X=X+1

40 PRINT 2*X^2+3*X+4

50 END
```

LET numeric variable name = numerical value

When a LET statement is executed, the value on the right side is calculated and substituted into the variable indicated by the variable name on the left side. In line 30 of Example 3.3, the value plus one is substituted into the variable.

Other variables can be used in the same way. Lines 30 and on in Example 3.3 can be changed to the following:

    10 LET X=10

    20 PRINT 2*X^2+3*X+4

    30 LET Y=X+1

    40 PRINT 2*Y^2+3*Y+4

    50 END

Decimal BASIC is not complicated. However, variables are used differently depending on the programming language, and a mistake can lead to a completely different execution result, so be careful.

3.3 INPUT

* To substitute a value into a variable when running a program, use INPUT.

Example 3.4

```
10 INPUT A,B

20 PRINT A*B

30 PRINT A+B

40 END
```

When Example 3.4 is executed, the execution result window shown in Fig. 3.6 appears. As is shown in Fig. 3.6, the two variables A and B are entered separated by a comma, and when "OK" is clicked, the execution result appears. The window shows the result of entering A = 4 and B = 5.

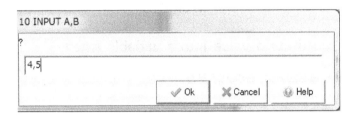

Fig. 3.6 Input window

3.4 PRINT

* Use the PRINT statement to display strings.

* By using the PRINT statement, you can control the format when outputting calculation results.

* When using semicolons to separate items, the execution results are displayed together for all items.

* When using commas to separate items, you can leave a space for each item to a specified digit.

Example 3.5

10 PRINT "KLM"

20 PRINT "Tokyo"

30 PRINT 2/3

40 PRINT 1;2;3

50 PRINT 1,2*3,3+5

60 PRINT "3+2 =";3+2

70 PRINT "Decimal"; "BASIC"

```
80 END
```

The pattern shown in line 60 of Example 3.4 is often used in programming.

4. FOR-NEXT(STEP), DEF, drawing graphs

4.1 FOR - NEXT(STEP)

* FOR and NEXT are commonly used commands. All lines between the FOR line and the NEXT line are executed repeatedly, whereas the value of the variable specified in the FOR statement is altered in turn. This pattern is often used in programming. The calculation of a series of numbers is outlined as its most familiar example.

Example 4.1 A program that applies n^2 to $n = 1, 2, 3, \cdots 10$

```
10 FOR n=1 TO 10

20 PRINT n,n^2
```

30 NEXT n

40 END

In Example 4.1, the lines between line 10 and line 30 are repeated to the point where n = 10. You can obtain a good understanding of this by executing this operation stepwise.

Problem 4.1 Write a program that calculates $1^2 + 2^2 + 3^2 + \cdots + n^2$ entering natural number n using the keyboard.

In Example 4.1, the value of the variable changes for each number from one to ten in increments of one, but you can assign a different incremental value.

*Using STEP, you can set the value added to the control variable when repeating the FOR-NEXT construction to any number different from one.

Example 4.2 A program that calculates the square of x of values from zero to one that increase by 0.1.

10 FOR x=0 TO 1 STEP 0.1

20 PRINT x,x^2

30 NEXT x

40 END

If required, STEP can be assigned a negative value. Try this for various FOR ranges and STEP options.

4.2 DEF

* This is used to define functions.

Example 4.3 We calculate the function $f(x) = x^3 - 2x + 2$, changing the value x by 0.2 increments from -5 to 5.

```
10 DEF f(x)=x^3-2*x+2

20 FOR x=-5 TO 5 STEP 0.2

30 PRINT x,f(x)

40 NEXT x

50 END
```

The function is defined in line 10, and the calculation is performed from line 20 onward.

Problem 4.2 Calculate x for the function $f(x) = (x + 1)^2$ by increments of two from -5 to 5.

4.3 Graph drawing

* Using the graphic function, you can draw function graphs. Naturally, you have to define the function for which to draw a graph, and set the range and grid of the graph window.

Example 4.4 A program to draw a graph for the function $y = x^3 - 3x + 2$ with a range of $-4 \leq x \leq 4$ and $-4 \leq y \leq 4$.

```
10 DEF f(x)=x^3-3*x+2

20 SET WINDOW -4,4,-4,4

30 DRAW GRID

40 FOR x=-4 TO 4 STEP 0.1

50 PLOT LINES: x,f(x);

60 NEXT x

70 END
```

For Example 4.4, the function to draw a graph is defined in line 10. The range of the graph window is set in line 20 indicating, from left to right, the minimum value for the x axis, the maximum value for the x axis, the minimum value for the y axis, and the maximum value for the y axis.

The graph window must be set within the graph range. The next line, line 30, sets the grid for the graph window. If no grid is required, line 30 can be omitted. Lines 40 to 60 contain the graph drawing task, and because these are repeating tasks, FOR-NEXT is used. The PLOT LINES in line 50 plot the graph using the function (Fig. 4.1).

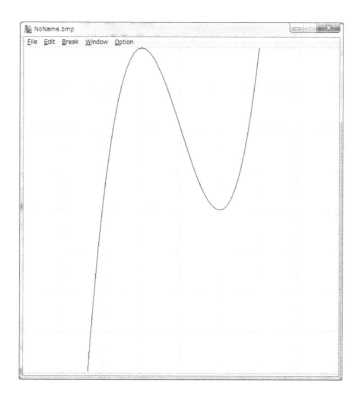

Fig. 4.1 Graph execution window

If you want the graph you have drawn to be easily printed or saved, you can select the required option from the File menu For instance, selecting File → Print displays the window shown in Fig. 4.2. Enter your printer settings in this window, and select "Print" to print the graph.

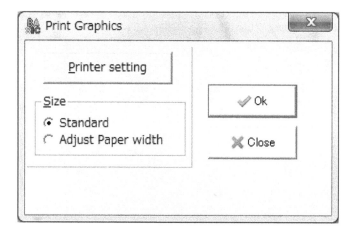

Fig. 4.2 Print settings window

5. DO-LOOP, DO-WHILE-LOOP, DO-UNTIL-LOOP, EXIT-DO

The same FOR-NEXT repeat execution explained in the previous chapter can be run with DO-LOOP and the other loops explained in this chapter. These are not limited to Decimal BASIC, and as the use of these types of loops is often seen in other programming languages, we recommend you becoming familiar with such loops.

5.1 DO-LOOP

* This is used to describe repeated processing.

Example 5.1 Infinite loop

```
10 LET x=0

20 DO
```

30 LET x=x+1

40 PRINT x

50 LOOP

60 END

In this program, the loop between lines 20 to 50 is repeated. In line 30, the value x is updated in increments of one.

Try this with various numbers. Click Break → Break in the execution window to display the Debug window shown in Fig. 5.1. By selecting "Cancel" and clicking "OK" , you can cancel execution. Naturally, by selecting "Step" or "Go on" , you can execute the program stepwise or continue execution. Try to use the Debug window in several ways.

Fig. 5.1 Debug window

Problem 5.1: Write a program with an infinite loop in increments of five starting from zero.

5.2 DO-WHILE-LOOP

* This repeats execution until a given condition is satisfied. The loop continues infinitely in Example 5.1; however, the DO-WHILE-LOOP is used when you want such a loop to continue until a desired condition is satisfied.

Example 5.2 Display the numbers from one to 50

```
10 LET x=0

20 DO WHILE x<50

30 LET x=x+1

40 PRINT x

50 LOOP

60 END
```

In this program, the loop between lines 20 to 50 is repeated, but only until the condition described after WHILE in line 20 is satisfied. Try this with various conditions and updating increments for x in line 30.

5.3 DO-UNTIL-LOOP

* This repeats execution until a given condition is satisfied. This loop is used in the same way as DO-WHILE-LOOP, with only a small change in the way the condition is inserted.

Example 5.3 Display the numbers from one to 50

```
10 LET x=0

20 DO UNTIL x>=50

30 LET x=x+1

40 PRINT x
```

50 LOOP

60 END

The program Example 5.3 has the same objective as the program in Example 5.2, but the condition in line 20 is described differently. Both ways are equally fine to use in programming.

5.4 EXIT-DO

* This is a command to move control to the line that follows the LOOP statement when the condition is satisfied during repeats of DO-LOOP.

Example 5.4 A program that matches an answer to a question.

10 PRINT "How many sec for a 1min ?"

20 DO

30 INPUT n

40 IF n=60 THEN EXIT DO

50 PRINT "Sorry, Try again"

60 LOOP

70 PRINT "CORRECT!"

80 END

In Example 5.4, the lines between lines 20 to 60 are a loop that is repeated until the condition in line 40 is satisfied. When you run the program, the input window for the INPUT command and the execution result window appear. Enter your answer to the question and click "OK". The question is repeated until the correct answer is entered.

Problem 5.2: In a program that displays the numbers one to 50 as described in Example 5.4, write a program that, after displaying 25, ends the loop and shows the text "stop displaying at 25".

6. IF-THEN (END IF), IF-THEN (ELSE, END IF)

6.1 IF-THEN(END IF)

* Executes only when a given condition is satisfied.

* Does not do anything if the condition is not satisfied.

Example 6.1 A program that displays the text "a is larger than b" if, upon entering a and b, a is larger than b.

```
10 INPUT a
20 INPUT b
30 IF a>b THEN
 40 PRINT "a is larger than b"
50 END IF
```

```
60 END
```

The IF-THEN statement in line 30 of Example 6.1 is used in all programming languages, and thus, it is extremely useful to become familiar with it.

6.2 IF-THEN(ELSE, END IF)

Example 6.2 If the condition is not satisfied in the program in Example 6.1, the condition that follows ELSE is displayed.

* Using ELSE allows you to determine the action to execute when the IF condition is not satisfied.

```
10 INPUT a

20 INPUT b

30 IF a>b THEN

40  PRINT "a is larger than b"

50 ELSE

60  PRINT "a is smaller than b"
```

70 END IF

80 END

The >= sign is used in place of the greater-than sign (≧) in setting conditions as described in Example 6.2. An action is added in line 60, following the ELSE line, to be executed if the condition in line 30 is not satisfied.

Example 6.3 A program that displays the largest of a, b, and c when entering the numbers a, b, and c using the keyboard.

>b THEN

30 LET large= a

40 ELSE

50 LET large =b

60 IF c> large THEN

70 LET large= c

80 END IF

In lines 20 to 50 of Example 6.3, "large" is assigned to the larger of a or b. Large is a variable to assign the maximum value. In lines 60 to 70, "large" and c are compared, and if c is larger than "large", "large" is assigned to c. In line 100, "large" is displayed.

Problem 6.1 Write a program that lists numbers a, b, and c, entered using your keyboard, in order from high to low.

Example 6.4 A program that determines whether there is a quadratic equation solution $ax^2 + bx + c = 0$ for entered coefficients a, b, and c.

```
10 INPUT a,b,c
20 LET D=b^2-4*a*c
```

```
30 IF D>=0 THEN

40  PRINT "solutions are available"

50 ELSE

60  PRINT "no solutions"

70 END IF

80 END
```

Students are quite familiar with quadratic equations, and whether a solution exists can be determined with the program in Example 6.4. The conditional expression is defined in line 20, and whether a solution exists is determined in lines 30 to 60 using IF-THEN-ELSE. Try to confirm the existence of a solution to other quadratic equations.

Problem 6.2 Write a program that displays the solution to quadratic equation $ax^2 + bx + c = 0$ for entered coefficients a, b, and c.

Example 6.5 Write a program that does the following: confirm the existence of a solution to quadratic equation $ax^2 + bx + c = 0$ for entered coefficients a, b, and c. If a solution exists, draw a graph of the equation. Graph range: $-4 \leq x \leq 4$ and $-4 \leq y \leq 4$, increment 0.1.

```
10 INPUT a,b,c

20 DEF f(x)=a*(x)^2-b*x+c

30 LET D=b^2-4*a*c

40 IF D>=0 THEN

50 SET WINDOW -4,4,-4,4

60 DRAW GRID

70 FOR x=-4 TO 4 STEP 0.1

80  PLOT LINES: x,f(x);

90 NEXT x

100 ELSE

110  PRINT "no solutions"
```

```
120 END IF

130 END
```

Example 6.5 contains several of the commands that have been explained to this point. A large number of commands must usually be employed in general programming. However, if you gradually master more such commands, you can write complex programs.

7. Built-in functions, CASE, defined strings, str$()

7.1 Built-in functions

A large number of functions exist in Decimal BASIC that is extremely easy to use when utilized properly. Those types of functions exist in all programming languages, but it is difficult to remember them all. When writing a program, various calculations and conditions have to be set. It is important to investigate on those occasions if appropriate functions exist.

General

General functions mainly encompass functions that perform mathematical calculations, for example, extracting the required part from calculations, abstracting symbols, etc. Try some calculations in a program. Example 7.1 shows a simple example.

Example 7.1 Obtain the absolute value for -53

10 LET x= ABS(-53)

20 PRINT x

30 END

ABS(x)   **absolute value for x**

SQR(x)   **non-negative square root of x**

INT(x)   **greatest integer not exceeding x**

MOD(x,y)   **remainder when x is divided by y**

CEIL(x)   **the smallest integer equal to or greater than x**

IP(x)   the integer part of x

FP(x)   the fractional part of x

ROUND(x,n)   the value of x rounded to n digits

Exponents and logarithms

Useful functions exist to calculate exponents and logarithms. For instance, when you have drawn an exponential function graph, you can easily build a program using EXP(x). Example 7.2 is a simple example of this.

Example 7.2 Obtain the common logarithm of 100.

```
10 LET x= LOG(100)

20 PRINT x

30 END
```

EXP(x)   exponential function

LOG(x)   natural logarithm

LOG2(x)   logarithm to the base two

LOG10(x)   common logarithm

Trigonometric functions

There is also a great need for trigonometric functions when building programs. Here, angles need to be substituted with radians. Look at Example 7.3, where PI indicates Pi.

Example 7.3 Obtain Sin (30°)

```
10 LET x= SIN(PI*30/180)

20 PRINT x

30 END
```

SIN(x)   sine function

COS(x)   cosine function

TAN(x)   tangent function

CSC(x)   cosecant function

SEC(x)   secant function

COT(x)   cotangent function

ASIN(x) θ where $\sin\theta = x$ ($-\pi/2 \leq \theta \leq$
$\pi/2$)

ACOS(x) θ where $\cos\theta = x$ ($0 \leq \theta \leq \pi$)

ATN(x) θ where $\tan\theta = x$ ($-\pi/2 < \theta <$
$\pi/2$)

ANGLE(x,y)   the angle between the straight line that connects the origin and point (x,y), and the x-axis (forward direction) ($-\pi < $ ANGLE(x,y) $\leq \pi$)

Hyperbolic functions

These functions can be used to obtain hyperbolas when programming. Its usage is shown in Example 7.4.

Example 7.4 Obtain the hyperbolic sine of zero.

```
10 LET x= COSH(0)

20 PRINT x

30 END
```

TANH(x)   hyperbolic tangent

SINH(x)   hyperbolic sine

COSH(x)   hyperbolic cosine

Random numbers

You can use this function to obtain pseudorandom numbers.

RND   pseudorandom numbers, $0 \leq \text{RND} < 1$

Example 7.5 Program to obtain pseudorandom numbers.

> 10 LET x= RND
>
> 20 PRINT x
>
> 30 END

Time

A function that can be used to display time and that shows the elapsed time since midnight.

Example 7.6 Program to obtain the elapsed time since midnight of the same day.

> 10 LET x= TIME
>
> 20 PRINT x
>
> 30 END

Other

Various functions other than the ones described in the previous sections exist, and one example of those, MAX(a,b), is explained here. The programs used in this guide to this point compare numbers using ">" and "<" in order to select the larger value of two numbers, but the larger number can also be selected easily using the function MAX(a,b).

Example 7.7 A program that extracts the larger of two numbers.

```
10 LET x= MAX(3,4)

20 PRINT x

30 END
```

MAX(a,b)   extracts the larger of a, b

MIN(a,b)   extracts the smaller of a, b

PI   approximation of π

MAXNUM   the largest positive number that can be displayed

Example 7.8 For y = (x + 1) / (x² + 1), enter integer a and integer b using the keyboard (a < b). When changing x by increments of 0.1 between a and b, the program shows the value of y, integer part of y, decimal part of y, value of y rounded to two digits below the decimal part, and the square root of y rounded to three digits below the decimal part.

10 INPUT PROMPT Please input "a": a

20 INPUT PROMPT Please input "b": b

30 DEF y=(x+1)/(x^2+1)

40 PRINT "y", "Integer part of y", "Decimal part of y", "Value of y rounded up to 2 digits below the decimal part", "Square root of y rounded up to 3 digits below the decimal part"

50 FOR x= a TO b STEP 0.1

60 PRINT y, IP(y), FP(y), ROUND(y, 2), ROUND(SQR(y), 2)

70 NEXT x

80 PRINT

90 END

PROMPT in lines 10 and 20 in Example 7.8 is a command to display the strings from the keyboard in the input window.

7.2 CASE

* Use this command when operations branch out. When multiple operations exist in a program, this function allows the selection of the required operation.

Example 7.9 A program that selects and calculates the absolute value and square root of an entered number.

```
10 INPUT PROMPT "Insert a digit": x
20 INPUT PROMPT "Select function?(1: ABS,
   2:SQR)": f
30 SELECT CASE f
40 CASE 1
50 PRINT ABS(x)
60 CASE 2
70 PRINT SQR(x)
```

```
80 CASE ELSE

90 PRINT "No action except 1 or 2"

100 STOP

110 END SELECT

120 END
```

In Example 7.9, the bifurcation is defined in line 20. Only two branches are defined in this case, but this number can be increased as necessary. The branches are selected in line 30. The first branch is executed in lines 40 and 50, and the second branch in lines 60 and 70. When the program is executed, the window shown in Fig. 7.1 appears. When values are entered in this window, the window shown in Fig. 7.2 appears. In this window, the task that is executed using one or two must be selected according to the definition. If you enter anything other than one or two, the message "No action except 1 or 2" appears, and this is an operation in lines 80 and 90.

Try a program that can perform various operations using this idea of bifurcation.

Fig. 7.1 Window 1 when executing

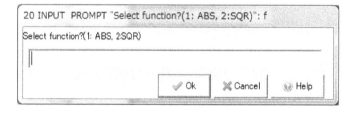

Fig. 7.2 Window 2 when executing

Problem 7.1 Write a program where, after entering positive integer a using the keyboard, you can select and draw graphs for the square root of a versus a when changing the values from 0 to a by increments of 0.1, and the natural function for a versus a.

7.3 Defining and connecting strings

Strings can be defined using the k$, s$ format. Such format is used when there is a need for defining strings when writing a program.

Example 7.10 A program that combines two strings.

```
10 LET k$="University of Science"

20 LET s$="Tokyo"

30 PRINT s$ &k$

40 END
```

In Example 7.10, the two strings defined in lines 10 and 20 are combined in line 30 and displayed. The format works similarly to defining variables. Example 7.10 can also be changed to the following format, where, similarly to variables, k$ is updated in line 20.

```
10 LET k$="University of Science"

20 LET k$="Tokyo" &k$

30 PRINT k$

40 END
```

7.4 str$()

* Use this function to change numbers to a string.

Example 7.11 A program that displays the value 25.456 as string 0.45625

```
10 LET x= 25.456
```

20 LET a= IP(x)

30 LET b =FP(x)

40 LET k$= STR$(b) & STR$(a)

50 PRINT k$

60 END

In Example 7.11, the integer part and the decimal part from 25.456 are extracted in lines 20 and 30, respectively, and these are converted and combined into a string in line 40.

8. External function definitions (recursive function, external subprogram)

When writing a long program, it is easier to divide the program into a main program and subprograms. The functions described in this chapter obtain the subprograms executed within the main program, and are the same in any programming language. Such a manner of programming may seem complicated at first, but once you become familiar with these functions, you will realize that they are extremely useful.

8.1 Recursive function

* The action of a function calling itself within its definition is referred to as a recursive call.

Example 8.1 Calculate a factorial using a recursive call.

```
10 DECLARE EXTERNAL FUNCTION fact

20 INPUT r

30 PRINT fact(r)

40 END

50 EXTERNAL FUNCTION fact(r)

60 IF r=0 THEN

70 LET fact=1

80 ELSE

90 LET fact=r*fact(r-1)

100 END IF

110 END FUNCTION
```

Lines 10 to 40 in Example 8.1 form the main program, and lines 50 to 110 form the subprogram. In line 10 of the main program, an external function is defined. In lines 60 and 70 of the subprogram, the factorial for zero is calculated, and between lines 80 to 110, the factorial is calculated when the value is different from zero. Because a recursion of r times is presented in the definition in line 50, line 90 is r*fact(r-1).

Example 8.2 A program that calculates the total from one to the larger value of two positive integers entered with the keyboard.

```
10 DECLARE EXTERNAL FUNCTION f

20 INPUT a,b

30 PRINT f(a,b)

40 END
```

```
50 EXTERNAL FUNCTION f(a,b)

60 LET k=MAX(a,b)

70 FOR t=1 TO k

80  LET total=total+t

90 NEXT t

100 LET f=total

110 END FUNCTION
```

In Example 8.2, lines 10 to 40 are the main program, and lines 50 to 110 are the subprogram. The subprogram is defined in line 10. When entering two integers in the main program, the larger value is determined in line 60 of the subprogram, the totals are calculated from one to the larger value in the lines 70 to 90, and this substitutes the defining function in line 100.

Problem 8.1 Write a program that calculates the total for the minimum and maximum value of three integers entered using the keyboard.

8.2 External subprogram

* The rules are virtually identical to the one described above, so it will be relatively easy to understand.

* Graphic formats cannot be changed in subprograms.

Example 8.3 Drawing a line connecting 2 points (1,1) and (3,3).

```
10 DECLARE EXTERNAL SUB lin
20 SET WINDOW -4,4,-4,4
30 DRAW grid(1,1)
40 SET POINT STYLE 4
50 SET POINT COLOR 1
```

60 PLOT TEXT ,AT 3,-0.5: "X"

70 SET TEXT ANGLE PI/2

80 PLOT TEXT ,AT -0.5,3: "Y"

90 CALL lin(1,1,3,3)

100 END

110 EXTERNAL SUB lin(a,b,c,d)

120 PLOT LINES :a,b ;c,d

130 END SUB

In Example 8.3, lines 10 to 100 are the main program, and the external subprogram is defined in line 10. The external subprogram is the portion between lines 110 to 130. In line 30, the grid width is set, which is one for this program. Point style and point color are set in lines 40 and 50, respectively. Line 60 is a command to display X near the x-axis in the graph at the location of point (3, -0.5). Lines 70 and 80 are commands to display Y near the y-axis, and line 70 is a command to turn the display 90° .

A line is drawn in line 120 based on data given in line 90. Use the external subprogram to work with the various programs that you have learned to this point. Also, try to display strings in various locations in the graph.

Problem 8.2 Write a program that draws a circle with a radius of three centered on point (2,1), and using the idea of a subprogram.

Example 8.4 A program that draws a line that connects points (1,1) and (3,3), and draws a circle with a radius of three centered on point (2,1).

10 DECLARE EXTERNAL SUB lin, cir

20 SET WINDOW -6,6,-6,6

30 DRAW GRID

40 CALL lin(1,1,3,3)

50 CALL cir(2,1,3)

60 END

70 EXTERNAL SUB lin(a,b,c,d)

80 PLOT LINES :a,b ;c,d

90 END SUB

100 EXTERNAL SUB cir(p,q,r)

110 FOR i=0 TO 360

120   PLOT LINES :COS(i)*r+p, SIN (i)*r+q

130 NEXT i

140 END SUB

Using the idea of a subprogram as shown in Example 8.4, multiple operations, such as drawing a line or drawing a circle, can be performed. In Example 8.4, the external subprograms are defined in line 10. Lines 70 to 90 show the external subprogram for drawing a line, and lines 100 to 140 show the external subprogram for drawing a circle. Because this idea of external subprograms exists in all programming languages, we recommend that you become familiar with it.

9. Handling data (read, write)

9.1 Handling existing data in programs

* BASIC has syntax for describing data in a program.

* DATA statements describe data separated by commas.

Example 9.1 A program to display the numbers one to ten in two rows.

```
10 DATA 1,2,3,4,5,6,7,8,9,10

20 FOR i=1 TO 5

30  READ a,b

40  PRINT a,b

50 NEXT i
```

60 END

The program in Example 9.1 describes the data in line 10. The data are read in the loop between lines 20 to 50, and displayed again. Such data are read through the READ command in line 30, and displayed in line 40.

Example 9.2 A program that describes and displays strings.

```
10 DATA
    "Tokyo","Osaka","Sapporo","Yokohama",
    "Nara","Hiroshima","Fukuoka","Kumamo
    to","Kagoshima","Sendai"

20 FOR i=1 TO 5

30 READ a$,b$

40 PRINT a$,b$

50 NEXT i
```

60 END

The content of Example 9.2 is approximately the same as that of Example 9.1, and the DATA command in line 10 describes the data you want to display in the program. Then, the program reads and displays the data from line 20 onward.

9.2 Reading data on a PC and displaying them

* Decimal BASIC allows you to read and process data contained in text files (TXT), and output the results as text files.

* Such data are easy to handle because they can be read using Notepad or another word processing software.

* If written in a text file similarly to input responses in INPUT statements, data can be

entered consecutively from the file. Normally, an input response that matches a singular execution of the INPUT statement corresponds to one line in the text file, but by separating such data with commas at the end of a line, you can write singular input responses over multiple lines.

Example 9.3 A program that enters and displays data that have been saved in a folder called DATA.txt created on the C disk of a PC.

```
10 OPEN #1: NAME "C:\DATA\DATA1.txt"

20 FOR i=1 TO 5

30  INPUT #1:s$,n

40  PRINT s$,n

50 NEXT i
```

60 CLOSE #1

70 END

The file called DATA1.TXT contains the four lines of strings and numbers, separated by commas, displayed after this paragraph. Naturally, you can increase the number of lines, but remember to set the FOR range in line 20 of the program correspondingly.

"Y", 7

"N", 9

"S", 10

"O", 7

In Example 9.3, line 10 defines the file where the data are saved on the PC. Be sure to specify the destination correctly. In line 30, the data from the saved location are entered in order into the program.

9.3 Writing to PC disk and reading from disk

* Data are written using WRITE. To read those written data using a READ statement, RECTYPE INTERNAL needs to be specified, and the file needs to be opened in an internal format.

Example 9.4 A program that writes data on the C disk on a PC as an EXEL file.

```
10 DATA "Yamada", 44, 7

20 DATA "Kiyohara", 34, 81

30 DATA "Asao", 35, 43

40 OPEN #1: NAME
    "C:\data\sample1.CSV",RECTYPE
```

INTERNAL

50 ERASE #1

60 FOR k=1 TO 3

70 READ s$, x,y

80 WRITE #1: s$,x,y

90 NEXT k

100 CLOSE #1

110 END

When executing the program in Example 9.4, the program writes the data indicated in lines 10 to 30 to the destination shown in line 40. Because this destination varies depending on the PC, set an appropriate write destination for your PC. If the write destination already exists, its data are deleted in line 50. In lines 60 to 90, the data in the program are read and written to the write destination on the PC.

In Example 9.5, data can be read from the write destination, and then displayed.

Example 9.5 A program that reads data from a PC write destination.

```
10 OPEN #1: NAME
   "c:\data\sample1.CSV",RECTYPE
   INTERNAL
20 FOR k=1 TO 3
30  READ #1: s$, x,y
40  PRINT s$,x,y
50 NEXT k
60 CLOSE #1
70 END
```

In Example 9.5, line 10 specifies the location where the data exist on the PC. In lines 20 to 50, the data are read from this specified destination and displayed.

10. Exercises

Question 1. Write the execution results of the following program.

LET A= 2.25

LET B= 100

PRINT ROUND (SQR(A),1)

PRINT (IP(A))^3, FP(SQR(A))

PRINT LOG2(IP(A))

LET C= LOG10 (B)

PRINT LOG2(C)

PRINT C/SQR(B)

PRINT MOD(B,8)

PRINT SIN (PI/6)*COS(PI/3)

```
PRINT (TAN (PI/4))^3

PRINT CSC(PI/2)+SEC(0)

END
```

Question 2. Write the execution results of the following program. Write the results for two windows, indicate the grid of the graph window, and only use black as the color.

LET N=10

let j=0

SET WINDOW -2, 10, -2, 20

DRAW grid(1,1)

SET POINT STYLE 4

SET POINT COLOR 1

for i = 1 to N

  LET j = i*2

  PRINT i, j

  PLOT POINTS: i, j

next i

SET TEXT COLOR 1

PLOT TEXT ,AT 4,19: "グラフ"

PLOT TEXT ,AT 4,-1: "Integer X"

SET TEXT ANGLE PI/2

PLOT TEXT ,AT -1,10: "Y"

END

Question 3. Fill the blank spaces (numbers ① to ⑤) to complete the program that draws a circle with a radius of three centered on point (2,1), and a rectangle that encloses that circle.

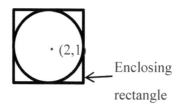

Enclosing rectangle

DECLARE EXTERNAL SUB circle

DECLARE EXTERNAL SUB box

SET WINDOW -6,6,-6,6

DRAW grid(1,1)

CALL box(①)

CALL circle(2,1,3)

END

EXTERNAL SUB circle(a,b,r)

OPTION ANGLE DEGREES

FOR k=0 TO ___②

  PLOT LINES:___③_____;

NEXT k

___④

EXTERNAL SUB box(x1,y1,x2,y2,x3,y3,x4,y4)

PLOT LINES: x1,y1;x2,y2;x3,y3;x4,y4;x1,y1

___⑤

Question 4. Write the execution results of the following program.

```
DATA 1,2,3,4,5,6,7,8,9,10,11,12

FOR i=1 TO 3

   READ a,b,c,d

   PRINT a^2-1,b/2,MIN(A,C),MAX(B,D)

NEXT i

END
```

References

[1] http://hp.vector.co.jp/authors/VA008683/

www.ingramcontent.com/pod-product-compliance
Lightning Source LLC
Chambersburg PA
CBHW070837070326
40690CB00009B/1591